RAILROADS

RAILROADS

DON BALL, JR.

NEW YORK   W. W. NORTON & COMPANY   LONDON

Published simultaneously in Canada by Penguin Books Canada Ltd.,
2801 John Street, Markham, Ontario L3R 1B4

The text of this book is composed in 10/13 Berkeley Oldstyle Medium
Composition by Zimmering & Zinn, Inc.
Printed and bound by Dai Nippon Printing Co., Ltd., Tokyo, Japan
Book design by Hugh O'Neill

FIRST EDITION

Library of Congress Cataloging in Publication Data
Ball, Don.
Railroads
1. Railroads—United States.   I. Title.
TF23.B349   1985   625.2′0973   85–4965

ISBN 0-393-02236-6

W. W. Norton & Company, Inc., 500 Fifth Avenue, New York, N.Y. 10110
W. W. Norton & Company Ltd., 37 Great Russell Street, London WC1B 3NU

1 2 3 4 5 6 7 8 9 0

To Karl Wiemer

I've got to be careful, for ours was, and continues to be, a very special relationship. Sure, Karl is like a brother, but it really goes beyond that. We've shared a lifetime friendship, and perhaps more important, a special world that few, if any, would understand. When we talk and laugh about grinds on Nepperhan Avenue, the pot and Colonial, and, of course, beaters, tears of laughter and memories flood back; when Conneaut or Corrinth or (Mrs.) Covington would come to mind, so does the laughter—and you can be damn sure we'd do it all over again! Karl and I have shared hundreds of hours together in locomotive cabs, and even had "our own B&O S-1." And, of course, I should say that we became noted for smoke and cinders on the CPR! Why, a 4000 to us is not a Big Boy, and certainly 3039, along with 3014 and 3017, are not New York Central Mohawks—for that matter, not even locomotives, though they are dear to our hearts. And Karl, should I mention Tabor or Briggs? Krummel and Tram? Should I throw in Steve's brief case? The Crisco? What about Fottage's sugar? Ray Anthony's "At Last" and Nat Cole's "Unforgettable" were very much a part of our lives, as was Pitzer's Buick, the Ford convertibles (best place to eat herring), the "VXIGBC," and the T-50. And yes, I should throw in the Barge, and Ridgecrest. Karl and I do have our differences: like the R-1820 versus the R-1830 aircraft engines; perhaps our biggest difference, though, is the fact that twelve drivers to Karl means an A, while to me, a 4-12-2. No matter, ours were rich years in a great America we love and still look for vestiges of. Well, this "brief" paragraph has obviously been written for you, Karl, even though you ain't!

SWEET SOUNDS OF SPRING! I am easily bothered by unnatural noises such as trucks, chain saws, motorcycles, and the like, but I make an exception here. And that is for the wonderful putting purr of a tractor in the field in springtime; the farmer turning the earth, following up and down the long furrows, in his annual ritualistic renewal of faith in the land. It is comforting that in this rapidly changing country the farms still stand out on horizons, or sit comfortably on the land, as the modern world whizzes past. Watching the farmer and his tractor, I ponder the fact that the work goes beyond the boundaries of dawn and dark, and the changing seasons. Certainly, the work is uninterrupted, hard, necessary, and rewarding—perhaps not in cash, but in living. Thoughts turn to July's sweet corn; yesterday's snowy mantle of winter is gladly forgotten. Spring's a time of coming alive, and what better place to witness life than on a farm!

I notice the greening of the willows, and see that the redwing blackbirds and the robins have returned. I feel the wonderful southerly breeze that carries the fragrant memories of other times. On both sides of the broad Connecticut River, the Vermont and New Hampshire hills rise gently, one melting into another in folds of green valley and sloping pasture, pushing upward into steep woodlands and rocky ledges. The majestic, lonely, shouldering outline of Mount Ascutney stands to the north. Just two hundred feet away is the main line of the Boston and Maine Railroad, and I am waiting, camera in hand, for an excursion train from Boston. As I wait, I delight in turning to other years. How easily I return to 1955 and a chase by car, next to these largely unchanged farms and rails, of a storming Central Vermont 700 series 2-10-4 on a freight out of White River Junction to Brattleboro! And as I stand and wait, I'm prepared for No. 72 to show, with its usual maroon and gold F-units and mix of B&M and New Haven cars. It takes little imagination to hear the approach of No. 72's diesels with the familiar-sounding 567s being let out on the tangent track. For that matter, a pair of Canadian National Fairbanks-Morse cab unit diesels (which replaced the CV 700s) heading a CV hotshot would certainly do the trick for me. I can picture the 35-mm slide of the yellow and green diesels in this perfect spring setting. But this is 1982, the Fs and F-Ms are gone, and in this SD40-2/Amtrak world, the train I am waiting for is a push-pull affair; an unusual purple, yellow, and silver-mist MBTA weekend excursion train that normally conveys commuters in and out of Boston during weekdays.

Behind me, over the fresh-turned black earth, and through the trees, the Connecticut River sparkles in the sun, a dancing diamond. I hear a distant air-horn and, once again, Boston & Maine E-units in maroon, Moguls in black, and 700s in smoke are as close as separated pages of calendars. My Canon is set: 1/500th of a second at F4.5, exposure No. 8 on a 36-exposure roll of Kodachrome 64. The anticipation of the approaching train is exhilarating, but the sight of the rapidly approaching F40PH diesel admittedly is a momentary letdown. All thoughts turn to getting *the perfect picture* of this train! In a brief few moments, the excursion train passes and is soon out of sight, approaching Bellows Falls. I have photographed a passenger train in daylight, on

rails that host only two Amtrakers in the darkness of the wee small hours. I will soon be adding a slide to my collection of unusual, rare (the commonly accepted rail-buff photographer's term), or out-of-the-ordinary train shots. There is no doubt that the Massachusetts Bay Transportation Authority train was well worth the wait. Lovely is the blue sky, and the green-yellow willows that complemented the train's gaudy colors.

As I drive back home, I know I will feel a little foolish, trying to justify the time spent away—and at the same time a little guilty over enjoying the sweetness of the springtime countryside alone. The railroad memories that came back were, as always, well worth the time at trackside.

This album reproduces some of the thousands of 35-mm transparencies taken at trackside since 1952. It is a "publisher's choice" of pictures, selected from slides that I submitted for consideration. I have indicated my preferences, and will briefly comment on a few favorites. I must also say that this book begs answers to many questions I raise of myself, about color photography, since I have always considered myself a "practitioner of conventional documentation"—that is, a black-and-white photographer. When going through my color material for this book, it became obvious that my interest in color paralleled developments and changes in the railroad scene. Item: some of my earliest photographic efforts were with Kodacolor, right after the war when there were so many brightly painted diesels heading our nation's passenger trains; somehow black and white just couldn't do. As I got older, and was able to purchase better cameras and build a darkroom, I needed black and white to capture the drama of the steam locomotive's last years, almost totally ignoring the diesels. And now with the colorful streamlined diesels gone, along with the regular-service steamers, I prefer to include more of the *total railroad scene*, and in color. Before getting into more thoughts and comments on photography, and the inevitable "color-versus-black-and-white-versus-color" question, it might be helpful to cover a little of the railroad history that occurred during my lifetime, and its profound effect on my photography.

The changeover from steam to diesel locomotives has been well documented—and lamented —in hundreds of books and magazines. I will preface my remarks by stating that in previous books I criticized the diesel for its lack of personality. Indeed, I have gone as far as to say that steam was *the color of railroading* and, in jest, that "a diesel is a diesel." Many years have passed since some of these remarks were made and a whole new generation of rail fans has come on the scene, a generation that missed the colorful early, streamlined diesels. It is not unusual to hear them argue that the zenith of locomotive design came from either EMD or Alco (that's Electro Motive Division of General Motors and American Locomotive Company). Nor is it unusual for them to argue that Alco's PA was better lookng than the EMD E-unit (or vice versa)—and they're talking diesels! It wouldn't be out of line, I suppose, to say that the colorfully painted early diesels might have played as important a role in luring color photographers to trackside as the technical advances in color photography did. In any case, a brief review of diesels and "dieselization" is in order.

In the first quarter of this century, America's railroad scene was strewn with the remnants of early diesel ventures begun with high hopes and lofty visions; visions, I should say, that ended in a total rout by the steam locomotive. As early as 1911, GE was sending engineers to Europe to look into the possibility of applying diesel power to the railroads, but it was not until 1924 that Ingersoll-Rand, GE, and American Locomotive Company joined forces to construct and deliver the first commercially produced diesel locomotive to the Central Railroad Company of New Jersey, for switching service. By 1934, the road to dieselization had begun—sort of—with over 400 diesel locomotives in service on our nation's rails. As I say, sort of. Every one of these diesels was tucked away on a dock, or on an industrial spur, or in a railroad yard somewhere, usually out of sight. All were small, boxy affairs, painted in various shades of black, as if not to upstage the ranks of black steam locomotives that ruled the rails.

On April 18, 1934, the curtain went up on diesels when Burlington took delivery of the first Diesel-electric streamlined train, built by Budd and powered by GM, *Pioneer Zephyr*. (And take note, "diesel" suddenly rated a capital "D"!) Nothing on rails ever looked like this sleek, low, dazzling, stainless-steel train. The *Zephyr* went on a national tour before entering regular service. Shortly after, the silvery train made a well-publicized dawn-to-dusk dash from Denver to Chicago, breaking all existing speed records. The Union Pacific soon followed suit, taking delivery of its yellow and brown M-10000 Diesel train known as the *City of Portland*. Like Burlington, the Union Pacific put its new train on tour, through "wind sprints," breaking many speed records. In quick succession, several more Diesel-powered trains such as New Haven's *Comet*, Boston and Maine's *Flying Yankee*, and Gulf, Mobile & Northern's *Rebel* took to the nation's rails—and the public's fancy. Coincidentally, Kodak test-marketed and introduced its first Kodachrome film during this same period.

By 1937–1938, the first true production-line diesel locomotives capable of handling existing heavyweight trains were built by the Electro Motive Division of General Motors for passenger train service and delivered to the Baltimore & Ohio Railroad. The Santa Fe ordered twelve identical units, and the Burlington ordered four—all to replace steam. Gone would be the made-to-order custom-built Diesel trains for individual railroads. From now on, it would be up to the styling department at EMD to create paint schemes and colors for the production look-alike diesels that would emerge from the erecting floor at LaGrange.

EMD was the new boy on the locomotive-building block, but old competitors were in the wings. True, EMD was diesel and nothing else, from the erecting floor up, but American Locomotive (Alco), in the locomotive-building business since 1848, wasn't going to let EMD run away with the potential diesel passenger train market. In 1941, Alco teamed up with GE and introduced its DL-109 passenger train diesel to compete with EMD's passenger Es. Both builders squared off on the

rails, and in slick printed ads and publicity. Meanwhile, the much heavier freight trains remained in the knuckled grip of the steam locomotives.

But by 1940, all-diesel EMD had enough locomotive-building experience under its belt to take on the steam locomotive in this greatest theater of operations, the freight-hauling business.

In early 1940, EMD rolled out its first diesel locomotive specifically designed for road freight service. Known as the 103 (its production number), it was a four-unit, 4,500-horsepower affair also called an FT. It had a streamlined cab on each end, or A unit, with two straight B units sandwiched between. Unlike the longer, sleeker production passenger diesels, each of the 103's units was a scant 50 feet—all four totaling 193 feet. Every wheel and axle was powered, unlike steam. That was the major difference. The guys at EMD's LaGrange plant really didn't know what they had gotten themselves into when they built the 103—whether it could do the heavy work that steam was handling let alone hold up under the stress and strain of freight service. Well, the rest is history. Once the 103 hit the rails, it not only bewildered those who believed in steam, but utterly amazed the designers and builders who had created her! 103's brilliant performance was marred only by strewn brawbars when veteran steam engineers backed their trains up to take up slack (out of habit) when starting a train. EMD's FT freight diesels proved they were ready to square off against the steam locomotive on every railroad, on any track, in any service. After the war, Baldwin and Fairbanks-Morse would enter this hotly contested mainline diesel market, but would never catch up with EMD, or the distant second-place runner, Alco. EMD's achievement in establishing itself as *the diesel locomotive builder* was acknowledged by a wave of imitators that never caught up. I find it ironic that Alco's PA seemed to be a favorite for publicity stunts using special trains—the Freedom Train and Power for Progress Train come to mind; likewise, articles in *Popular Mechanics* and *Life* magazine—yet EMD was getting the orders!

Each diesel builder, like automobile manufacturers, designed their own streamlined "car body" shell to cover the innards of the diesel's machinery, and while chief mechanical officers found truth in numbers and in performance, the "sex appeal factor" of the various diesels also played a very important part in selling one over another. Each diesel locomotive builder's design and styling staffs came up with different body shells and paint schemes so as to promote distinctive messages of appeal not only to potential owners but to the general public.

The steam locomotive's individual identity as manufactured for each railroad was the result of designing and building a functional machine to the specification of a particular railroad's mechanical requirements. The fact that most steam locomotives were adorned with a coat of universal black paint did not detract from their honest individuality. On the other hand, with the new mass-produced diesels, the railroads suffered a loss of identity, but saw a chance for a new *color identity*, and the result was a riot of painted zigzags, arrows, stripes, vees, cannonballs, and the like, on the billboard-sized car body shell. In many cases, paint schemes "worked" and the railroads became famous as a result of their colorful diesel engines and train names. In some cases, such as with Santa Fe's "warbonnet" paint scheme, the visual results were so successful that the mass-produced piece of machinery imbued a personality to the railroad itself, just as the steam locomotive had earlier.

Just as surely as diesel devotees have their favorite paint schemes, they also have their favorite diesels—the Alco PA and EMD's E units generally regarded as being the most popular. There is no question that EMD has been the leader in number of locomotives produced, but to the "non mechanical types," the "sex appeal factor" seems to be the main reason for one diesel being favored over another. There are several examples of the big Alcos and EMDs in this volume, so let's take a look. Let's look at Santa Fe's big Alco PA, poised in Los Angeles Union Passenger Terminal—hot off the *Grand Canyon Limited*—aloof, and wrapped in disciplined elegance. From every angle, the no-nonsense PA possesses unflagging good taste and non-negotiable integrity, yet the onlooker does not have to be high-brow to appreciate its honest, yet stylish sheet-metal lines. The PA leaves no doubt about the fact that it is a machine to be admired and respected. What about EMD? Well, Alco's "big" 2,000-horsepower PA diesel is commanding, stately, and massive, yet, ironically, it is 5 feet shorter than its "not-so-massive" EMD counterparts. Alco's square-flanked PA is a yacht that rides on arrestingly handsome 15-foot, 6-inch trucks— truly an example of distinguished design that stands out among its peers. Take a look at the Alco PA (or its smaller look-alike FA freight diesel brother); a vote of confidence is definitely in order.

But what about EMD? What about the fact that EMD's sculptured metal snout from the 1930's has functionally endured into the 1980s? EMD's E-class and F-class diesel locomotives smack of restrained luxury and structural logic, with their smooth metal skins drawn tightly down over their noses. The EMDs combined slipstream stability with maximum visibility. There is no conspicuous misuse of chrome, and the sculptural modeling of the body shell isn't superfluous, but related to the basic machinery underneath. I have always been impressed by the seemingly aesthetic effectiveness of the efficient design on, and around, EMD's bulldog snout. It endures.

I have talked about the generous, graceful curves of an EMD cab unit, as well as the "executive authority" of the Alco PA and its look-alike FA brother. I have not mentioned the other locomotive builders' interesting, often laughable designs that never quite measured up to Alco and EMD—oh, maybe Baldwin's sharknose diesels notwithstanding. Some of these units are pictured throughout the volume, so you be the judge. In the late 1940s, when we had Buicks and Chryslers, few would pay real attention to the Kaisers and Studebakers.

Sadly, and while steam was being replaced in the 1950s by newer, utilitarian, second-generation road switcher diesels, so too, the earlier streamlined cab diesels were being retired in favor of the newer, general purpose diesels. The few cab units (and passenger trains) remaining were, in most cases, eventually given simplified paint schemes in order to cut down on the costs of masking and painting. Why, a New York Central passenger diesel without its flashy silver trucks and racy lightning stripes was not worthy of heading the Great Steel Fleet. And what was Rock Island, undressed of crimson, silver, and maroon! Atlantic Coast Line dropped its flamboyant purple, gold, and pearl (along with thirty-four painters) in favor of a somber black and delux yellow. Missouri Pacific's diesels were painted solid blue and their eagles lost their chrome-colored wings. So too, Pennsy's elegant pin stripes came off and Chicago Great Western's beautifully painted diesels went solid red—as did the whole railroad!

By the 1950s, as people drove V-8 Chevys and flew Connies in ever-increasing numbers, the flashy, colorful diesels were no longer needed. For that matter, the trains they hauled were not needed either. First there were steam and heavyweight passenger cars, then diesels and lightweight streamlined cars, then a jet-conscious America. . . . I am reminded of Houston Union Station in 1960, when the Boeing 707 was entering airline service. There were thirty-six passenger trains in and out of Houston each day. Missouri Pacific had twenty-two of them; Santa Fe, eight; and Burlington and Rock Island, the remaining six. "The *Twin Star Rocket* is now departing on track . . ." By 1967, *three* passenger trains arrived in and departed from Houston Union Station. At railroad stations throughout America, bumper posts militantly stood at tracks' ends—silent reminders of glamorous days now gone. "Your attention, please! The *Texas Eagle* is now departing on track. . ." From far off in a railroad yard, a locomotive horn stirs memories. The silence in the station remains. The horn sounds again; this time I listen more carefully—it is a dirge to the end of an era. "The *Texas Chief* is now departing on track . . ."

Fitting for the close of our discussion of diesels is the subject of paint schemes. Was there a "most popular" or "most successful" paint scheme? In terms of the successful use of linear paint decoration that emphasized the form of the diesel's car body, I would certainly nominate Erie's and Lehigh and New England's Alco FAs for top honors. But what about the *most popular* paint scheme? This, of course, is sensitive, subjective ground—like the looks of Alcos and EMDs. It really boils down to which scheme did *you*, or do *you*, like? (And I'm reminded of Varga's paintings of "classy chassy girls" that used to adorn *Esquire* magazine during the years the most colorful paint schemes adorned diesels. Surely, everyone's favorite was his "patriotic gal" pin-up!) Without a doubt, when we're talking about diesel locomotives, well, Santa Fe's dashing red and yellow "warbonnet" paint scheme judiciously applied on silver—EMD or Alco—achieved the distinction of being the most popular among diesel devotees. I have to go along with the majority on this one, which explains the disproportionate number of Santa Fe diesels appearing in my books.

As is quite evident from my other books, I seem to be inflicted with the joys and memories of childhood, and a more simple or less complicated life. I learned at an early age that in a split second—a *split second!*—a moment can be preserved: a moment sensed, enjoyed, photographed, and hopefully, caught at the right time by the camera. Successfully producing images that I can share as visual statements of my excitement and love for something photographed is the criterion, as far as I'm concerned, for the truly successful photograph. It is easy today—really, almost foolproof in some cases—to take a technically excellent picture with today's automated cameras. But, does the photograph express the "intended feelings" of the photographer? Ansel Adams states that "the photograph represents something perceived and deeply felt—the equivalent of an emotional or aesthetic experience."

Here's where I stick my neck out on films, and my rather simplistic view of them. My first axiom: When you've found a film you are happy with, stick with it! Sure, there are fast films, slow films, warm films, cold films, and everything in between. Try them all out; get to know them, and then stay with the one you like. For me, that's Kodachrome 64 for color, and Kodak Tri-X (120) for black and white. And, yes, if I *have to* use a tripod in poor light with the 64, so be it. If the subject is in poor light and moving, sometimes it just isn't worth wasting the film. I feel that the shots I *can get* with Kodachrome 64 make up for those I can't get. And I might add that my remarks are based on my own satisfaction with the color rendition of K-64, coupled with my preference for documentary photography. What I say is based solely on my experience preserving something that I see, on film. When I do get into a discussion about films—which ones look "brassy," grainy, are harsh, or soft, render the truest blues, reds, etc.—I simply go back to which film does the best job for what I'm trying to do with the camera. Axiom No. 1, if you will.

Now, while we're on the subject of color films, I'd like to share a few personal thoughts on slide (transparency) films and their chronology in my life, starting in 1951 when I received my first slide camera for Christmas. Kodachrome film, which was introduced to the market in 1935, was the generally accepted choice when I got my new Pony camera. It seemed as though everyone I asked was using Kodachrome. With an ASA of 10 (and my F4.5 lens), there were many "off-color days" when friends would be able to shoot using their better lenses, while I could only watch. Of course, when the sun was out, the Kodachrome colors were fabulous (but within a year I went to a faster shutter and better lens). In 1955, Kodak came out with Ektachrome High Speed (ASA 100) Professional film. I bit, but felt that the depth and rich warmth of the Kodachrome were missing. Perhaps, in retrospect, the Ektachrome rendered "more realistic" blues, greens, and blacks, but I had gotten used to the deep, rich hues of Kodachrome. In 1956 I tried Anscochrome, hoping for a film that would offer the higher-than-10 ASA plus "better color"; this proved to be a disastrous mistake, and back to Kodachrome I went! In 1959, Kodak placed its High Speed Ektachrome on the market. By then, I was shooting a lot of 120 color transparencies with my Rolliflex, and the Ektachrome film offered the most satisfactory results for me. (Strangely, when shooting 35-mm slides, I still preferred the Kodachrome over the Ektachrome.) In 1961, the finest film to date, in my opinion, was introduced—Kodachrome II.

With an increase of 2½ times the speed over the original Kodachrome to an ASA of 25, and with a definite improvement in sharpness and detail in shadows, this film, again, in my opinion, became the standard by which others would be judged. In 1962, Kodachrome X was introduced with an ASA of 64, and many of my friends switched over to it. I tried 35-mm rolls of Kodachrome X over the next few years, especially on "bad weather outings," but always returned to Kodachrome II. In 1974, both Kodachrome II and Ektachrome X were replaced by K-25 and K-64, respectively. For me, it was a heartbreaker losing Kodachrome II—regardless of what Kodak and their ad agency said. Back and forth I went, shooting both K-25 and K-64, usually having to expose both films for an ASA of 40 and 80, respectively, to try to enrich the colors. In bright sunlight, the new Kodachrome was unforgiving in its harshness. In one exposure—with either film—I found it impossible to get details in deep shadows, if "accurate color" was to be obtained in the sunlight. Whenever I overexposed for slight shadow detail, the rest of the colors would tend to wash out. Without sun, however, both of the new Kodachromes seemed to "zap up" the color, "improving" otherwise dreary lighting in many cases. Today, I feel this still holds true, and consequently my preference for shooting color in other-than-high-noon lighting. Axiom No. 2 might be: *Never shoot color in direct sunlight between 11:00 A.M. and 2:30 P.M.*

I have since settled for K-64, and although I do not know what Kodak has done to improve the film, I find it much more satisfactory these days (but I still need to underexpose it slightly to enrich and strengthen the colors.) As I said earlier, Kodachrome II, in my opinion, *was* the film by which others would be judged. Though the film is extinct, the statement stands.

On May 1, 1971, the National Railroad Passenger Corporation was formed to take over the operation of our nation's inter-city passenger trains. On that day, 178 trains rolled into history, leaving just 182 trains operating over 20 participating railroads. What individuality there was to a passenger train soon blended into Amtrak—the red, white (well, it's called "platinum mist"), and blue generic passenger train. Almost overnight, the last few streamlined passenger diesels disappeared from their assignments and, for many of us, interest in rail photography diminished—as it did when steam disappeared from the rails. As a matter of interest, the loss of steam had turned many of the old guard—black-and-white photographers—away from trackside, while the colorful streamlined diesels had attracted a new breed of color photographers. Now, with mainline scheduled steam gone—along with those colorful diesels—well, a whole new generation of railroad photographers can be seen at trackside continuing the documentation of the railroad scene.

How many times do we say, "There always has to be a last. . . ," and how many times is "that last whatever" virtually ignored until it is either endangered, or doomed? There always is a "last," and in the second decade of Amtrak passenger trains, the Rio Grande Railroad is the maverick that continued to operate its own passenger train, rather than join Amtrak. Long ago, I learned about a "bird in hand. . . ." But the Rio Grande was two-thirds a continent away, and besides, I had gotten used to passenger trains being Amtrak. Somehow, the Rio Grande and its own passenger train were another world to me.

The *Rio Grande Zephyr!* Unsung to this writer—until close to the end. The *RGZ*—America's last privately operated intercity passenger train; a one-of-a-kind rolling museum in today's Amtrak passenger train world. Considering the fact that I have a son who rode the Union Pacific and Santa Fe to and from California before the advent of Amtrak, but barely remembers it (he has since logged thousands of miles on Amtrak); considering that I have a daughter, born right after Amtrak, who loves "picture book passenger trains"; and considering their dad, who models Frisco E-8s and Rock Island Fs, and just about any passenger train that ran in and out of Kansas City in a world of pre-Amtrak passenger train memories, it was time for the family to experience the *Rio Grande Zephyr,* before it, too, became memory. So the *Rio Grande Zephyr* it was—the silver survivor of the famous *California Zephyr*; the train that defied Amtrak and held on to the past. The *Rio Grande Zephyr,* reachable by car, Continental Airlines, a limo, and a Denver hotel! *Rio Grande Zephyr*—unbelievably my last chance to share the once common, privately operated passenger train with my family.

Now, allow me to digress a little about the *Rio Grande Zephyr.* In 1949, and before superhighways and 707s, the Burlington Route (Chicago to Denver), Rio Grande, and Western Pacific (Salt Lake City to Oakland/San Francisco) inaugurated the famed *California Zephyr* to travel their three railroads between Chicago and California. Unlike competitors Union Pacific and Santa Fe, the *CZ* was scheduled as a "cruise train," with a slower schedule. While Santa Fe and Union Pacific tried to keep their Chicago-to-California service to under forty fast hours, the *California Zephyr* was deliberately slowed to a schedule of approximately fifty leisurely hours to allow passengers to view the Feather River Canyon and Colorado Rockies in daylight. Each of the three railroads operating the *CZ* bought a slew of Budd-built stainless-steel vista-domed cars, the number divied up by a simple formula based on the number of miles the train would operate on each road. The Burlington furnished three train sets; the Western Pacific, two; and the Rio Grande, one. When the train entered service on March 20, 1949, it was generally advertised—and regarded—as the most beautiful train in the world. The *CZ*'s demise came when the Western Pacific dropped its portion of the run in 1970, claiming operating losses. When Amtrak took over the nation's passenger trains in 1971, maverick Rio Grande elected to keep Amtrak off its property and to continue to operate its own "mini-CZ" between Denver and Salt Lake City, known as the *Rio Grande Zephyr.*

When the Official Guide to passenger service was 2 inches thick, I never appreciated Burlington and lightweight stainless steel. My world was one of black Union Pacific steam locomotives, Santa Fe first-class streamliners, and Rock Island red, crimson and silver. Somehow, the Burlington wasn't on my list, and while I made sure I rode the *Chief* and *Golden State,* the *California Zephyr* remained familiar only in

ads, and on chance encounters between Chicago and Denver. The Rio Grande and Western Pacific railroads, which operated the *CZ* with the Burlington, were even further removed from my "hands-on" train-riding and train-chasing experiences. So now, riding in a taxi down Seventeenth Street in Denver to Union Station to ride the *Rio Grande Zephyr* struck me as being a bit awkward. But as is so often the case, memories of other trains and other times abounded. I remembered savoring the taxi cab rides to Dearborn, Chicago, to catch the Santa Fe; likewise, to LaSalle to board the Rock Island west or the New York Central east. But now, pulling up to the huge gray granite Denver Union Station with my family to catch the *Zephyr* was just not a comfortable fit. For one thing, I did not want to be disappointed. I wanted my kids to see (and, I hoped, to understand) why I used to be so excited about being on board a passenger train. I reminded myself that it was 1983. Would it still be possible to experience the individuality of a railroad in a passenger train?

After paying the taxi fare, my son mentioned that he saw some "yellow diesels" just before we pulled up to the station. "On a passenger train?" I asked. "I don't know, I only caught a quick glimpse." It was decided we'd all walk around the north side of the big station to take a quick look (for a moment, I felt as if we were avoiding the Sacred Mosque in Mecca, not entering through the front doors.) There, between the umbrella canopies, was a postwar F-9 diesel lashup, headed by the A unit #5771, caught in the morning sunlight, resplendent in gold, black, and silver, coupled to a vista-domed streamliner—a one-of-a-kind survivor from a thousand yesterdays: the confident familiar chant of 567 engines idling away; the baggage wagons being unloaded into the baggage car; the smell of breakfast being prepared in a diner named "Silver Banquet"; and a gleaming silver train that looked the way it did when Budd built it in 1948. With the complete and total demise of the American railroad's passenger trains, this lovely gold and silver train struck me as something God had forgotten to abandon! I savored every foot of what I saw, but the thought of how lucky we once were to have had so many beautifully individual trains ran over and over through my mind. "This is the way it used to be," I choked out to my family.

At 7:10 A.M., we boarded the elegant *Zephyr* and took first-row seats up in the spotless dome of "Silver Bronco," a 1948 Budd-built coach. All around the station and train was the normal hub-bub of activity that accompanies the departure of a great train—the way I remembered it to be. Looking from the dome, the gleaming train struck me as intrinsically part of the vast station scene; I was looking for passenger trains of the Union Pacific, Rock Island, and Burlington . . . the tracks were all empty. I knew that anyone who remembered the *California Zephyr,* the *Rocky Mountain Rocket,* or the *City of Denver* was right at home.

It's 1983 however. We take a long look at those F-9s up ahead, on the head of the *Zephyr,* with their confident 567s chanting away. To the casual observer, they look very much like a "gold and silver 103." Certainly those sixteen cylinders, arranged in a 45-degree "V"-type block in each diesel unit are the same basic powerplants as in the 103. Our three F-9s are nothing less than elite survivors of the 7608 F-class units that followed the 103 into service on our nation's railroads, north, south, east, and west. Like the train she is coupled onto, she is living history.

Back on April 28, 1940, at this same station—maybe this same track—EMD's mainline freight demonstrator 103 was preparing to show nonbelievers what Diesel really was.

Diesels were built for switching and, more important, for the colorful new high-speed passenger trains that were hitting the nation's rails and capturing the public's fancy. Diesels appeared in ads for the new passenger trains in *Holiday* and *Life*. They graced the covers of timetables and slick booklets the railroads printed to promote their glamour trains. Those of us who made railroading our hobby soon got to know Diesel engine numbers and paint schemes; specifically, which Diesels usually hauled what passenger trains where and when. As always, the freight trains moved behind steam, and we usually knew which class of engine handled freight on what part of the railroad. There were always too many steamers and freight trains to know *their* engine numbers and which one ran where. On April 18, 1940, the guys at Electro Motive in LaGrange, Illinois, were in the process of changing all of this. Indeed, though they did not realize it at the time, they were in the process of changing the very heart of railroading itself, once and for all.

Those of us who ventured down to the depot found that the big, glamorous passenger diesels had a presence much more real—gritty and railroady—than in the retouched color ads in magazines. We could see that their stamina certainly transcended their colorful images in the magazines and booklets. Some of us were surprised, yes, totally caught off guard, to see these glamour trains called upon to act. We quickly accepted the sleek diesels on the passenger trains.

In notably sharp contrast to the dashing passenger-train diesels, little was said about demonstrator 103 when it left the erection shops. Instead of the customary ballyhoo and hoopla that accompanied the passenger diesels, the 103 just rolled onto the properties of the various railroads that agreed to try her out on freight. In sharp contrast to the brightly painted passenger diesels, 103 appeared in drab green, with yellow stripes veeing down to the letters "GM" on the nose. No preaching the internal combustion gospel for freight trains, just a wait-and-see attitude by those aboard the diesel and, of course, the host railroad. As we await the departure of the *Zephyr*, I keep thinking about April 28, 1940; back to the roundhouse to join the boilermaker, who is staring grimly out of the back door toward the ready tracks and the long four-unit caterpillar-like diesel that somehow doesn't fit into the gritty surroundings of the railroad—or into the boilermaker's heart. The roundhouse foreman walks past, smiles distractedly, and goes to his office as other roundhouse workers gather. Almost as if tranquilized, they stare quietly at the 103—and (perhaps) their own futures. A pipe fitter eyes the 103 as if to say, "Go back where you belong, wherever that is." It is obvious that, to the uninitiated, this new

creature is as intriguing in its mystery as the steam locomotives are in their familiarity. The blackness of everything seems almost an affront to the graceful lines and yellow stripes of the 103.

Incredibly, the group of grimy guys at the back door would soon find out that this well-drilled performer was capable of outperforming every steam locomotive the Rio Grande had! All cynicism would quickly be silenced by the 103's four 567-series V-16 engines, incredible 270,000 pounds of drawbar pull, lower operating costs, and almost 100 percent service availability. A closer look by the guys at the roundhouse would have shown that she was huskily seductive, placing all of her 4,500 horses and 400 tons on the drive wheels, where it counts.

103's tests on the Rio Grande projected the very essence of what this new FT diesel was all about—cresting Tennessee Pass at 10,200 feet, and not breathing hard, crossing Utah's hot, flat desolate desert at speed, and not stopping for water. The 103 went on to complete an astonishing 83,764-mile journey over twenty railroads in thirty-five states. Only *after* the 103's successful journey did the guys at EMD indulge in their success, having routinely put their freight Diesel on the line day after day. They had the right stuff.

Picture the 103 waiting confidently in Union Station, its 567 model engines chanting away in a four-unit ensemble that would soon depart over the Moffat route for Grand Junction—just as today's *Zephyr* is preparing to do. And those F-9s, up front, go right back to the 103! These diesels are absolute living testaments to EMD's calculated gamble, back in 1939, to produce, that is, *mass produce,* a diesel locomotive that would finally break steam's hold on freight railroading! Why, with just a little "paint and imagination," it is easy to visualize the brand-new demonstrator locomotive No. 103, painted in its cloak of dark green, trimmed in yellow with "GM" on the nose, and "Electro Motive" spelled out on the side, waiting for the highball.

Now we get the highball, and the drama of today's *Zephyr* begins.

In a short time, I head for the open vestibule door to get a look at the railroad, as we leave the mile-high city of Denver behind. Up front, the raging F-9s open up on tangents, only to encounter 10-degree turnback curves—clawing their way upward to get a footing on the Front Range. They open up on every straight piece of track, charging our ears with an infectious roar of 567 engines, which is one of the most satisfying sounds of railroading. Simply magnificent in this setting! I tell two obvious newcomers to the world of railroading that this is the way it used to be. They watch and listen to the 567s up ahead . . . . They have become initiated. The engines and train twist and turn, curve after curve, as if looking for an easy way up! The F-9 ensemble cooks through the first of twenty-eight tunnels, with their sure-footed familiarity and authoritativeness, into a tormented landscape of rocky escarpments, jagged ridges, and plunging cliffs. The diesel's hot, oily exhaust turns the image of the *Zephyr*'s silvery stainless steel to brown as we exit each tunnel.

The 567s continue to shout in almost ceaseless intensity with their full-throated exhausts—really restatements of what the 103 was all about, and of what 103 and EMD would do to change all of railroading.

During the 5771's vocal triumph up ahead, I was told she had logged well over three million miles since she was built in 1955. I headed back up to the dome for a better look at this command performance. I pondered all the implications . . . and I wondered if *anyone* back in LaGrange, back in 1955, on the erection shop floor, could have imagined what their newly created machines were destined to do! Wonderful, that EMD F units were still at the helm of the *Zephyr*—just as they were intended to be!

Time and space do not permit me to *really describe* the collective thrill that every one of us shared—safely surrounded by the glass domes, as we plunged in and out of tunnels, along ledges, past over-hanging rocks, and through giant fir trees, interspersed with breathtaking vistas of the Rockies. . . . Likewise, there was the wonder of having china, linen, and silver on the tables in dining car "Silver Banquet," where potatoes were still peeled and eggs fried in the 7×30-foot stainless-steel kitchen—out of which orange-coated waiters emerged with generous portions of meals comparable to the finest restaurants. Whether in the diner, a dome, or back in the observation car "Silver Sky," the *Rio Grande Zephyr* provided the opportunity to slow down, enjoy, and catch up with memories.

And, oh yes—the *magic* of the past; departing Chicago's Union Station behind silver E units, racing a sunset across table-top Illinois into Iowa . . . . the magic of Feather River Canyon, Keddie, the Niles Hills, and finally Oakland. We found the *Rio Grande Zephyr* to be very much in touch with the past—its silvery cars all members of an immortal cast. The *RGZ* was both a journey into the living past and a fitting monument to a period in railroad history when the sleek passenger train was the polished hallmark of the railroad company that operated it. The *Rio Grande Zephyr* was a fulfillment for me, and for my family.

If it wasn't for this book, I wonder if I would have even given thought to the fact that just about 90 percent of my shots taken on and from the *Rio Grande Zephyr* were in color! In another book, I talked about the convenience of that 35-mm camera—but 90 percent? Well, for one thing, the cost of color film and processing has fallen in relation to black and white. For another thing, all I do with color is buy the film, shoot it, and wait for Kodak to do the rest. Easy? And, I think of a comment I recently made to a friend who asked why I shoot something "colorful" in black and white. "Because I can do something with it in the darkroom!" was my answer.

I find color photography a lot more uncontrollable and un-forgiving than black-and-white film—the biggest factor being that color film cannot tolerate an error in exposure (though my batting average seems to be a good one). With black-and-white film, I can usually control the "lights and darks" when printing the picture. I can reveal detail in both dark areas and light areas by dodging, and burning in, the enlarger's light source when making a print. In effect, I can add "feeling" to a black-and-white print. So, does this mean that black and white is more "efficient" in the long run? That the 10 percent of all shots I took on the *RGZ* in black and white are a sure thing, versus the X percent of the color? With color, it's easy to keep the good shots and throw out the bad ones; but isn't it more fun, and satisfying, to be able to control "feelings" with black-and-white prints? Perhaps this is the place to mention a nagging, perhaps contradictory, approach I take with color photography in contrast to black and white. In *Rails*, which I consider the black-and-white counterpart to this book, I mentioned that I snubbed telephoto and wide-angle lenses. (Since writing that book, I have bought a Mamiya 645 with both an 80-mm *and* a 105- to 210-mm zoom lens for black and white.) For years, I have used a 90-mm lens and both a wide angle and a zoom for color. The simple reason was, and I think still is, that I can crop or compose with these lenses so that the color transparency is always a finished shot, instead of waiting to get into the darkroom to do the same with a black-and-white negative. Maybe West Coast photographer Ted Benson is right in his assessment that these lenses are tools for expression and not part of the matrix of thinking that goes into the "documenting" versus "creating" syndrome. And Lord knows, I think of the times along the South Shore Railroad with photographer and friend Joe McMillan, where we argued over and over about this. Well, guys, you've got me up over 200 mm, so perhaps we're making progress!

At one time, I strongly felt that the steel-on-steel adventure of railroading could only be portrayed in black and white—in tones of gray, contrasted with brilliant whites, cast against the starkest blacks. Power! might best describe this reaction to trains and railroading. Strength I could capture on black-and-white film; strength I could further enhance, in the darkroom, when making the print. My black-and-white images of railroading were compositions perceived in linear strength and form. At one time, color film was used only for "pure documentation" of the paint schemes on the early diesels, and for nothing else. A steam locomotive, besides "being black," and offering up shades of "gray smoke" and "white steam," was a complex subject that demanded the information and detail that only black-and-white could capture—or so I thought. As Ted Benson puts it, "black-and-white photography is the thinking man's medium."

But what about color? The idea of having to pit one medium against the other frustrates me. Suppose that by some freakish whim of nature all the color about us should suddenly disappear! What a drab world this would be. We would then appreciate—because of the lack of it—how much color really means to us. Think about it.

I feel that color brings greater realism to a picture. And black and white? I love it when shapes and forms and good balance are brought together into a "perfect," pleasing composition; and I realize that color can often distract from, or weaken, the simple and direct imagery of black and white. I honestly think I prefer color when the mood and scene are one of serenity, unusual light, and striking yet subtle contrasts—when there is mystery in the air (I should say lighting). Black-and-white photography gives raw-boned strength to a scene! Black and white is light and intensity, something I can control. Color is experience, something we naturally respond to, remember. Color, or black and white? If it were the 1940s and 1950s all over again, and we had the films and equipment we have now, I'd shoot the diesels in color and the steamers in black and white. Did I answer the question?

When I picked out a selection of several hundred slides for this book, it became very obvious that some of my favorites bordered on what I would term "monochromatic color." Looking over the slides I can only draw the conclusion that I prefer shooting color when the scene is subtle—the light soft or sometimes downright flat. As a matter of fact, most of my favorites were taken in adverse weather and lighting conditions, such as fog, snow, or twilight. Under this light, color film brings out the infinite variations of hues that otherwise tend to go flat in a black-and-white print. I find that in any diffused-light situation, what you see, especially nearby, becomes close and intimate, somehow offering subtleties of tone and color that are lost in black-and-white photographs. I am reminded of the time my friend Walt and I set up for a "perfect picture" of the ex–Texas & Pacific steam locomotive #610 on the Southern at Prophet, Virginia. The big 2-10-4 boiled up the rails under a billowing black cloud of oily smoke, and then under our vantage point from a wooden overhead bridge. "Wow!" was our joint reaction to the spectacle. Walt shot color and I shot black and white. A week later, I eagerly went into the darkroom with "that picture" fresh in my mind. When I printed it, there was no way I could separate the smokebox front, deep foliage, and black smoke; Walt's color slide was fantastic! In this particular case, and not getting into a dissertation on tonal values and hues, the color definitely "worked," whereas the black and white didn't.

I have walked miles and miles and ridden bikes and buses, ferry boats and trucks in my life-long pursuit of trains. I have worn out automobiles in the process. And each time I write a book, all of the train-chasing memories flood back to me—wonderful memories that make the efforts worthwhile. Perhaps the hardest thing for me to come to grips with is not only how much the world is changing, but *how fast!* What was commonplace a couple of decades ago is now gone!

In the fall of 1956, I was in the Ohio-Indiana-Chicago area chasing trains. Prior to embarking on my two-week trip from New York, a buddy sent me his itinerary for a train-chasing safari in the southern part of the Midwest, where the L&N and Central were still dispatching their finest-in-steam. I had opted for Pennsy and B&O lakefront operations in Ohio and, perhaps more important, the New York Central out of Chicago. Now, keep in mind that this was a time when *total divisions* of major railroads were being dieselized overnight, and the hunt for steam was full of risk; even risk of arriving as close as a *day behind* the last scheduled run with steam. When I arrived in Chicago, I had missed New York Central steam—missed what I had routinely expected. I remembered my buddy's itinerary and wondered if he was faring better. A few blind calls to New York Central in the Cincinnati area told me he was indeed at the right place! I had covered five states in the past week, however, and was at the point where I needed a good night's sleep to keep going. I had run out of steam, myself. It was a Friday, and I had to be back in New York in four days; somehow, I *had* to get to the Queen City to see some New York Central (always a favorite) steam. After checking road maps and railroad timetables, I decided to fly down in the morning. Reservations were promptly booked on Delta's flight 749.

It seemed ironic at the time to be patronizing the very mode of transport that was responsible for the vanishing railroad passenger schedules. However, time is time, and I didn't have any! Besides, a confession is in order here; a confession long overdue. I was, and continue to be, a nut on piston-engine airliners and a flight on one was always a thrill—second only to the passenger train. Piston airliners have long since disappeared from the main trunk carriers, like the E units and F units, but their legacy lingers on feeder lines—just as a few remaining E units and F units do in commuter service and on branch lines. What was so common . . . what was taken for granted. . . .

There really *is* a similar development and life-use pattern between streamlined diesels and commercial airliners, albeit usually overlooked by any and all who write about the history of transport. I've always been fascinated in these almost totally overlooked, yet uncanny similarities in the development of both the diesel-powered passenger train and commercial airliners. Didn't the DC-3 make its debut and entrance into service just as the various three- and four-car streamlined trains took to the nation's rails? And didn't the big pressurized four-engine Boeing Stratoliner enter commercial service just as the first production passenger train E units were entering service? In 1946, when the F-unit really hit pay dirt with a backlog of railroad orders—and when the big Alco PA and newer E units *really* came on the scene—so, too, didn't the Douglas DC-6 go into production, with customers lining up, exceeding assembly-line capacity? As Fairbanks Morse and Baldwin got into the passenger diesel locomotive act, so did Lockheed, with its beautiful Constellation capturing a lesser number of orders than the DC-6, but garnering a greater amount of affection, just as the Alco PA did. Boeing's Stratocruiser, like Fairbanks Morse, was, to some, ahead of its time, yet just a little late onto the market (and I can compare the military application of FM's opposed-piston marine engine to the big, burly Boeing Stratocruiser, itself a commercial outgrowth of the B-29 Bomber—neither the Stratocruiser nor the FM diesel locomotives captured their share of the market). Refinements continued on the diesel locomotives and piston airliners as mass production of both was fine-tuned to meet the increased demand of the traveling public. Between 1949 and 1954, EMD started the development (along with Alco and others) of the boxy hood unit geep that would usher in a new era of diesel locomotive utility, replacing the aging, but graceful, streamlined cab unit diesels. During these same years, the airframe and engine manufacturers were developing and marketing turboprop aircraft that would ultimately usher in pure jets and replace the aging, but graceful, piston engine airliners.

The similarities between diesel locomotives and piston airliners are quite evident. Both were spawned into a silvery age of speed in the 1930s, gradually leading to innumerable improvements, refinements, and a great increase in power to handle more work. Like flight, the railroad's fundamental principle changed very little. Only the equipment changed.

On Saturday morning, I arrived at Midway airport, for the 9:40 A.M. flight, expecting to be boarding a DC-3, or possibly a much larger DC-6, for the quick, one-hour, flight to Cincinnati. When I arrived at the Delta ticket counter, flight 749 was posted on the departure board as *The Royal Poinciana,* with its destination being Miami. Under the pertinent information, it said "Golden Crown DC-7 service." Certainly not the DC-3 I had expected!

Now, being a fancier of piston-driven aircraft, I always preferred the DC-6b over the later DC-7. I felt the DC-6 was "more of an airplane," somehow; more stable and solid. The DC-7 was a rush against turboprops and the coming jets. And certainly the transcontinental, ocean-hopping DC-7 was to be considered the last of a breed of piston-driven transports that would someday challenge the jets. I had no complaints!

Departure time rapidly draws near, and I mentally run through some of the schedules of trains that I know, while reassuring myself that flying *is safe!* I ponder over the fact that hundreds—thousands!—of planes are now safely in the air right at that moment! I think of the millions of dollars that went into Douglas's and Lockheed's efforts to comfortably move people over the earth at speeds of 300 miles an hour and better. And yes, I *do* wonder where the *City of Miami* and *South Wind* are, and how many of their passengers wouldn't get on an airplane. My stomach tells me that no matter how exciting planes are . . .well, I'm entrusting my life to a machine that doesn't like land! But I remember my last flight, and I not only survived, but enjoyed it! Yes, I love the big planes—and sometimes have to remind myself!

The boarding announcement is made for flight 749 and we proceed toward the doors that lead to a world reserved for Connies, Martin 404s, DC-3s, Convair 240s, and the like. Hardly the atmosphere, or comfort, of, say, Dearborn or LaSalle. We bunch up and walk through the double doors to our gleaming DC-7. And, just as many of us do with PAs and E units, I start comparing the long, straight lines of our Douglas with a nearby TWA 1049 Super Connie—a three-finned man-made shark if there ever was one! Like the DC-7, the Connie is the end of the piston-driven airliners—both destined to be holdouts against the turboprop Viscounts, Electras, and, yes, the oncoming jets. Looking at the huge 3,250-horsepower Wright R-3350s with their four-bladed props, I am reminded that, like steam, and like diesel, the power of this machine is visible, whereas a jet's power is concealed.

In a few minutes, the door is shut from the outside, and the line man wheeling a fire extinguisher appears down below us, then under the wing somewhere. A cabin announcement is in progress, but so is the No. 3 engine, cranking away. After twenty blades or so, it fires up in a big sputtering cloud of smoke from oil residue, trying for an instant to shake any confidence we might have in flying. Number 2 is next, followed by 4, then 1. Soon 13,000 horsepower is running four polished propellers slashing through the air! There is certainly no turning back, changing minds, getting off, now! Another cabin announcement is made, pointing out that the *fasten seat belt* sign is on and that there is no smoking. "All seats must be in an upright position." We start to move, then commence to taxi out toward the active runway, the four shiny props reflecting their arcs around the inside of the cabin. Many of us listen intently to those R-3350s to make sure they "sound right." An American Airlines Convair 240 is ahead of us as we near the end of the taxi-way. The captain turns our big ship 45 degrees into the wind, while the Convair turns onto the active runway and starts its takeoff roll, past us. Each of our engines is run up in the same sequence as they were started, and the whole plane shakes and quivers, as if anxious to break ground. All control surfaces are checked for freedom of movement, and there is a tremendous increase in cabin noise as the Wrights fight the locked brakes. Similar to being in a locomotive cab, we are aware of the fact we are *surrounded* by machinery! Momentarily, all four engines quiet down and we taxi and turn onto the end of the long, straight runway. "Will the cabin attendants please prepare for takeoff?"

Once again, all four engines in this grand production are run up to about 50 percent power and the anxious Douglas shakes and shudders more than ever! The brakes are mercifully released this time, and we are gently—firmly—pressed into our seats as throttles are advanced to maximum power. The noise is tremendous! We rotate, in 29 seconds, and flight 749 is airborne, climbing away from the concrete runway. We roar across the airport boundary; houses and buildings are a blur out the window—streets are at crazy angles as we climb dramatically. For a brief moment, it feels as though we are going to be hurtled straight ahead, while the plane climbs! Hydraulic pumps whine, followed by the clunk of each gear locking into place. There really *isn't time* to be scared!—And I forgot to watch the gear retract. The hazy gray city falls away as we begin to ease back to our normal rate of climb power. I am not alone in fiddling with the air-flow control vent. There is another change in engine noise as the propeller pitch is increased to get a bigger bite of the air. Some passengers actually hold gently on to the curtains as the confident ship continues to climb, and I sense the collective relief of many who cannot take flying for granted. Soon we pass over the southern tip of Lake Michigan, and bump through some of the many fair-weather cumulus clouds that surround us. We then enter into bright sunlight and clear blue sky as we emerge from the blinding cloud tops. I watch those big Wrights out on the wing, grinding up the air, and enjoy a "Ranch Hand" breakfast brought to my seat. I *try* to contemplate the fact that I will soon be back on the ground, chasing New York Central Mohawks and Hudsons.

In 1956, Cincinnati Union Terminal, with its great variety of motive power, was a treat, but like great cities that also have their flaws, CUT had its share of flaws in 1956. The biggest one, perhaps, was not seeing a single example of New York Central's celebrated Niagaras—

certainly to be considered one of the finest steam locomotives ever built (some say *the* finest). Incredibly, older Mikes, Hudsons, and Mohawks were at Cincinnati, but the Niagaras were not to be seen. Indeed, we learned from a dispatcher that Central's oldest steam locomotive, a decrepit 2-6-0 built in 1900, was surviving—and operating yet—in Canada! Having a sympathetic railroad employee tell of the demise of a class of steamer was an all-too-common heartbreaker in the 1950s— but a New York Central Niagara?

The name of the game in the fifties was usually to let the most modern, certainly the best, steamers do battle with the diesels out on the railroad until time ran out. Logic would have it that the Niagaras would be the battlers for the Central. After all, we're talking about a locomotive that emerged from the erecting hall of American Locomotive on March 10, 1945, amid fanfare usually reserved for a visiting head of state We're talking about a locomotive that emerged amid speculation that here was the creature that would take on, and beat, the diesels. From brass bands to speeches, the Niagara was viewed that sunny March 10th as the very symbol of America's pride and power. Indeed, the locomotive was named Niagara "because of its great power," to quote then New York State Governor Thomas E. Dewey, who was a speaker at the ceremony. It was the Niagara that was built to run with the *20th Century Limited* and the other streamliners in Central's "Great Steel Fleet." It was the Niagara that routinely ran over 25,000 service miles a month—a record envied by other railroads. And it was the Niagara that could throw her tremendous 6,600 horsepower into the task of hauling freight, if called upon. No, the Niagaras were simply so good that there just wasn't a place for them on the less demanding runs that still drew steam in 1956. The fact that the Niagaras were gone was the best, certainly the most convincing, testimonial to dieselization to date, in my train-chasing experiences. It's a pity a Niagara wasn't saved in a museum—like the #6015, which was still sitting cold, up in Beech Grove, Indiana, destined to go to Luria Brothers for scrapping, while we were enjoying the show in and around the Queen City. On the Central, the final curtain would fall on the ordinary, amongst the ranks of steam.

Although I didn't really grasp the implications at the time, 1956 may very well have been *the* year of the greatest change(s) in the railroad industry. While Niagara #6015 was headed for Cleveland and Luria Brothers for scrapping, Union Pacific's last 4-12-2 #9000 was headed for California and a museum at Pomona. Chicago and North Western was closing out steam, while Reading and Santa Fe steamers were coming out of storage to help power-short Pennsy, which was waiting for delivery of the most massive order of diesels to date. Likewise, Illinois Central 4-8-2s and Burlington 4-8-4s were sent to pitch in on the Grand Trunk Western, which, like Pennsy, found itself short of power, waiting for new diesels. And Cotton Belt 4-8-4s and 2-8-0s headed west to help power-short Southern Pacific. Down on the Norfolk and Western, coal-turbine-electric *Jawn Henry* was busily at work, as if diesels didn't exist—yet at the same time, those Western Maryland 4-8-4s, built in 1947 and among the nation's newest steam locomotives, were lined up for the cutter's torch.

In 1956, diesels had even replaced the electrics on the Great Northern, where hydroelectricity was abundant. So, too, the first of sixty new revolutionary diesel-electric/electric FL-9 locomotives arrived on the New Haven from EMD to run diesel under the wires and electric under Park Avenue into Grand Central Terminal, eliminating the diesel-to-electric change of locomotives—and the pure electric locomotives, altogether. The concept of a true intermodal rail/highway trailer with steel retractable wheels and rubber retractable tires was introduced on the Chesapeake & Ohio. Low-center-of-gravity, lightweight passenger trains, such as Pennsy's Budd-built *Keystone,* Pullman Standard's *Train X,* and General Motor's *Aerotrain,* were introduced to our nation's railroads in an effort to help solve the problem of a $700 million yearly loss in passenger train operations. In 1956, Southern built and introduced a 92-foot-long freight car—albeit a box car— which would be the harbinger of today's jumbo cars. It was also in 1956 that the first private meetings were held to discuss the possible benefits of merging the giant Erie and Lackawanna railroads into one. And it was in 1956 that the New Haven Railroad started to really look into its Park Avenue real estate holdings to develop them into more viable properties.

Certainly tradition was broken—and, as we see today, a precedent was set—with the corporate identification of the New York, New Haven and Hartford Railroad Company into purely "New Haven" with its Barnum "NH" logo. This change occurred a year earlier, but it was in 1956 that the heavy press campaign started to change the look of a whole railroad! Ditto Monon, from the Chicago, Indianapolis and Louisville Railroad. And what about those colorful cab-unit diesels? Well, it was in 1956 that Western Maryland's steam era "fireball" Fast Freight Line herald went to "WM" speed lettering, and it was in 1956 that Chicago Great Western's simplified "Lucky Strike" logo replaced the elaborate "Corn Belt Route" herald en masse—let alone a solid maroon paint scheme in lieu of the elegant tuscan-maroon, red, and gold scheme. In 1956, Rock Island started a solid maroon paint program while New York, Susquehanna & Western replaced its maroon and gray with a grayish silver. The biggest change might have been the replacement of Pennsy's beautiful gold pin stripes in 1956 with a solid yellow stripe. Yes, it was certainly hard enough to photograph the diesels that replaced the cherished steam locomotives, and with the loss of the flamboyant paint schemes that individualized the mass-produced diesels, what little enthusiasm there was to continue railroad photography diminished.

To a great degree, the photographs in this book picture various aspects of what I call the "visual revolution" in railroading: the many changes that have taken place over the last three decades. While dieselization was, of course, the most noticeable visual change, the sharp-eyed photographer witnessed an industry besieged by change, from ties to signals. The diesel changed the very power structure of many a railroad, but the whole look of railroading—from welded rail and automated yards, to piggyback, hi-cubes, and Amtrak—changed the face of the industry in the time span covered by this book.

I know one thing: I love the "quiet understatements" of color that I cannot feel in black and white; subtle tones, such as the ochres, umbers, and siennas that appear on the side of rails and on wood ties—against the harshness of a polished railhead, or stone ballast. I think of the warm wood tones of the old Stamford freight house, with just a glimpse of the contrasting cool blue sky through the window. Likewise, the pleasant shades of rusty browns that adorn that lonely, forlorn New York Central boxcar sitting along the mainline, amid the cold wintry landscape of rural Indiana. The soft hues in these "quiet studies" add information and realism that I don't think I could find in black and white.

The cold strength of the dominating steel wheels of Steam-town's ex-Canadian Pacific locomotive #1246 contrasts with the blue clothes of the men who tend her, the color accentuating the warm tones of the grease. Certainly, the red grease bucket adds a contrasting focal point of color that I think would be unnoticed in black and white. Similar thoughts prevail for the cursed fiery hell of the cutter's torch, dismantling Union Pacific's steam locomotive #3332, the deadly flame of the torch contrasted in bright white-yellow against the almost black-and-white light of an already dreary day. When I compare this scene with my black-and-white shots, I find that the intense flame, in color, makes the horrifying experience very real.

Shooting from within a dark place, looking out into sunlight, is most striking in color. In many cases, I find that black and white will bring attention to the dark forms that frame such a picture, whereas color adds impact, directing attention to the main subject. I think of Union Pacific's yellow diesels on the *City of St. Louis,* viewed from within the Bonner Springs tower, rushing past on their westward trek. Certainly similar shots taken in black and white don't quite have the same feeling. The same applies for Chicago & North Western's *Pennin-sula 400* departing the dark confines of Chicago & North Western Terminal, heading into broad daylight. The attention is on the colorful train and not the shapes and forms of the darkened station.

Earlier I mentioned monochromatic color and adverse lighting conditions. What better time for my kind of color photography than in the midst of a heavy snow! Size and perspective often are lost in snow—and you get flat lighting—but the results can be dramatically exciting. Two scenes come to mind: The Santa Fe yardman thawing a switch in Argentine, Kansas, and the Amtrak GG-1 roaring through Noroton Heights, Connecticut. Consider what that fusee would look like in fair weather! The even quality of the light from the darkened skies and falling snow has greatly intensified its red flame. Ditto for the rondles on the signals at Noroton Heights. Even the solid black G is subdued, lending a little mystery to the scene. Black and white could be very satisfying in these conditions, but the color adds a little extra something. No doubt about it.

Color is definitely for cold snowy weather! I should say *adverse* cold, snowy weather, where, quite often, subtle and beautiful hues appear. Sure, that Green Mountain Railroad snow plow fighting more wind than snow came out well in black and white, but that hint of its

warm, weathered red paint only intensifies the cold! The same is true of that Belt Railway of Chicago Alco, working the Clearing yard in cold, miserable weather; I love the hint of yellow on the diesel, which serves to direct attention to the otherwise "black-and-white qualities" of the scene. Of course, it is the same for the winter scenes along the South Shore Railroad, where the orange appears all the more vivid against the snow.

Now, another thought on color as the "added ingredient." Take a look at Illinois Central's 4-8-2 Mountain type No. 2507, head on, at Kankakee. She's just the way I remember her—brown! I doubt that the tonalities in a black-and-white print could really describe her. The surface and color of the beautiful engine bespeak of the hues of the rails and ground over which she runs. The color again adds information, from soot to rust, that a black-and-white shot I took of her doesn't. Rather than simply document the 2507 as "just another black steam locomotive," the color introduces a feeling of intimacy—knowing the rich work stains of this machine. There is no doubt in my mind that color suggests more things to look at. After all, color is how we see!

My sense is that there are plenty of photographers out there who would not only argue with my prejudice for color under the circumstances I have mentioned, but could reason that black and white is better. I would love to have a counter-critique from, say, Bob Olmsted, Ted Benson, John Krause, Phil Hastings, Mel Patrick, and Jim Shaughnessy, just to name a few of my favorite railroad photographers who have stayed mostly with black and white.

Yes, I have to agree with Ted Benson, who finds color photography less demanding, or challenging, than black and white. And, as I've said before, in color photography, the color factor alone adds information about the subject. Undoubtedly the colors themselves become important compositional factors in a picture (and here *just may* lie most of the rationale for those who prefer color over black and white or vice versa).

Taking a quick look at composition, I have to go back to my own thoughts that I elaborated on in *Rails.* The "good photographer" who takes a "good picture" has first analyzed the scene and determined the "best way" to shoot the picture, *before* making the exposure. All of the elements in the scene are examined and organized in the view finder before the picture is taken! Two feet . . . six inches can make the difference between an ordinary picture and a good one! Look at what you want to photograph, then look at it through the viewfinder. The smallest change in camera angle can make a whale of a difference in the final picture! A simple rule I've established for myself is always to show scale (if possible) to the elements in the picture. In most cases, this means adding foreground information to indicate distance and add interest. Another "rule" I've tried to establish is never to place the horizon smack in the middle of the picture. With a looming train, "punching out of the picture," the horizon, of course, is little noticed. Just try to *avoid the obvious,* and place the horizon below or above, deciding whether the sky or ground is more interesting. The same applies, I would say, for placing the main subject right in the middle of the picture. Go to the left, or right, balancing the composition with space, or shapes, or color! If you look hard enough, there will be something to incorporate into your composition to make it more interesting. Think about it. Try it.

Finally, and perhaps most important, study the background and make sure it works with the subject (and sometimes this *does* mean placing the main subject smack in the middle—especially with portrait-type pictures). A wire behind something, or a telephone pole "growing out of something" can ruin the shot. *Think before you shoot!* The possibilities for a different, interesting, and satisfying picture are endless. It really all boils down to "feeling" what you have analyzed *before* taking the picture.

Well, now, color or black and white? Could the criterion be how much work you want to put into the final picture? Or how much control you need—perhaps to "add feeling" to the final photograph? Could the choice boil down to style, or commercial necessity? Could it be a matter of understanding objects in relation to each other or to the light that strikes them? Could it be individual preference or "taste"?

For example, I love the fact that, even though color film can show the full range of hues in a single shot, this does not mean that all of the basic colors must be present. In fact, as I've said, I love the monochromatic images and the greater impact a single source of light or brightness can, and will, give you. Perhaps by showing less, in color you are actually getting more! Color, if nothing else, adds information. But then again, I feel that black-and-white photography can be a greater challenge.

My photography is a result of my being an enthusiastic observer of things around me. Emotions can run the gamut from being awed by powerful shapes and forms to loving the softness of certain qualities of light. My reaction can sometimes be best expressed in color, and at other times in black and white. Photographs are, to me, simply documentations of how I see life and, to me, there is room for—really need for—both color and black-and-white photography.

In *Rails* I mentioned that photography is communicating what you see and perhaps more important, how you feel about what you see. In my opinion that still stands.

Always referred to as a "fifty hundred class" on the Rock Island, one of this fine family of 4-8-4s is pictured steaming into the Armourdale yards in Kansas City, Kansas.

The cold winter sky viewed through the warm, subtle tones of the weathered Stamford, Connecticut, freight house on the New Haven Railroad. *Opposite:* A close-up look at Illinois Central's handsome Mountain type 4-8-2 at Kankakee, Illinois. Wonderful that she has picked up the very colors of the land she runs over!

Long Island Rail Road's unique Fairbanks Morse C-Liner diesel is caught in the late afternoon sun at Jamaica Station, Queens, on an Oyster Bay train. *Opposite:* Before the gradual erosion of time, turnpikes, and trucks brought the once-prosperous New Haven Railroad to its downfall, the clean and still-proud *Yankee Clipper* rushes past a switch stand at Glenbrook, Connecticut, headed toward New York.

The late Lucias Beebe stated, "When [the] diesel came to demean alike the stature of the engineer and the wonderment of his machine, a long and honored legend was terminated." *Opposite*: The man and his machine in the personages of Union Pacific's Northern #8444 and engineer at Laramie, Wyoming. *Above*: The backhead of a Reading T-1 class freight locomotive.

Evening approaches and the setting sun envelops Hiram Walker's Brick plant in a warm glow, along with Peoria and Pekin Union's local freight finishing up its day's chores in Peoria, Illinois. *Opposite*: The study of New York Central's 131-pound rail near Scarsdale, New York, carries through the same warm hues, though taken early in the morning.

TICKETS
BAGGAGE

Opposite: The glass and steel latticework patterns over Pennsylvania Station's train concourse in New York City. *Above:* The former Wabash Railroad's *Banner Blue* making a hasty departure out of Chicago's Dearborn Station, dashing under Roosevelt Road for its new owner, Norfolk & Western.

Opposite: The stark black, angular shape of a Norfolk & Western SD40-2 diesel adds to the drama of the fast westbound freight roaring through the tranquil Blue Ridge back country near Elliston, Virginia. *Above:* In the pre-mechanized days when gandy dancers drove the spikes instead of machines, occasionally a misdriven one assumed a bent form resembling a piece of modern sculpture. The late afternoon sun glances through the trees, highlighting a little "modern art" along the tracks of the New York Central near Valhalla, New York.

Opposite: Santa Fe's daily local to Leavenworth, Kansas, rumbles onto the first of six 164-foot spans that will carry the train across the Kaw River from Wilder Junction into Bonner Springs, Kansas. The Union Pacific's Kansas division is in the foreground. *Above:* A platform view of the preparations at the head end of Erie-Lackawanna's *Phoebe Snow* prior to her departure from Hoboken Terminal for Buffalo.

Erie-Lackawanna E-8 diesels on the westbound *Phoebe Snow* open up on the tangent near Denville, New Jersey, passing a Hoboken-bound MU train in the process.

A study of the patterns of Lackawanna railroading at bumper post's end on the Erie-Lackawanna at Hoboken Terminal, New Jersey—the *Phoebe Snow*'s postwar daytime streamlined Pullman Standard equipment blending in nicely with the 1930-era Pullman Standard electric commuter cars.

Above: The rails come alive with the daily passage of Octoraro Railway's northbound freight headed toward Modina, Pennsylvania, with gons full of scrap steel. Spring has come to the historic Brandywine Valley back country of Delaware, and it is a time when the quality of light is soft and rich. *Opposite:* We are in California's great Tehachapi Mountains, where distant vistas are ever present. When shadows grow long and day is almost done, this magnificent outdoor amphitheater of harsh land takes on a gentle, almost etheral shroud of mist over its folds of hills, punctuated by the stately Black Oaks. The curving rails near Allard are temporarily quiet—though a distant train can be heard, assaulting the grade. Before it reaches our high trackside location, most of the light will be gone and the first stars will be appearing overhead.

Bread and butter for Vermont short-line railroads. Loaded 50′7″ boxcars assigned to newsprint service are seen heading south along the Central Vermont at Windsor, Vermont. That's Mt. Ascutney in the background. *Opposite:* Railroading is a seven-day-a-week, twenty-four-hour-a-day business—without a roof! Witness this Belt Railway of Chicago crew, working the vast Clearing yard, south of Chicago on a dreary, dismal Sunday.

40

Opposite: Darkness starts to fall over the quiet land near Lawrence, Kansas. Along the Union Pacific, a westbound freight approaches behind a 9000 class engine, slowing for a stopped train in Lawrence, taking on water. A mile to the west, and several seasons later, two Union Pacific switchstands catch the golden light of sunset. This part of Lawrence is flat, and the lovely gold-to-rose transition of light will last a few more minutes before the sun disappears, low on the horizon.

Rule 14 L in every railroad's book of rules clearly states that a train approaching a grade crossing must blow two long whistles, a short, and a long until the crossing is reached. *Above:* Changeless in outline over the years, the familiar "cross bucks" guard motorists from oncoming harm along the Octoraro Railway near Mendenhall, Pennsylvania. *Opposite:* Their locomotives now gone, these Chesapeake & Ohio Vanderbilt tenders stand in the weeds at Huntington, West Virginia—vivid reminders to some of better days, but now, merely equipment held for possible use by the railroad for water or oil service on work trains.

The invisible power of a diesel hard at work and the visible power of a steam locomotive are very evident on these two pages. *Above:* A handsome trio of New Haven's distinctive Alco FA diesel freighters growling through the rock cut at Poughque, New York, on the Maybrook line. *Opposite:* Burlington's Mikado-type locomotive #4960 moving through the crackling zero degree temperature in the railroad's Clyde yard near Chicago.

Two of Nickel Plate's famed diesel-racing Berkshires hammer out of Calumet yard on the south side of Chicago with fast-carded freight CB-12, their engineers screwing down the reverse gears, "hooking 'em up" for some mighty fast running east. In steam days, many have said the Nickel Plate was the fastest freight hauler in the business. I cannot verify this, other than to say that, on several occasions, I watched Nickel Plate freights from parallel New York Central passenger trains keeping up with us! *Right:* A quick grab shot of a New York Central P-motor, taken from the vestibule of a New York Central local-express (their term) from New York City to White Plains. The inbound train is *The Pacemaker* from Chicago, both trains passing on the Harlem River lift bridge between Manhattan and the Bronx.

Everyone has had a few of those "damned if you do, damned if you don't" days and Saturday, October 17, 1953, must have been one of them for a few guys on the Frisco. Train No. 111, *The Oklahoman,* left Kansas City for Tulsa promptly at 11:05 P.M. and almost made it out of town—almost. Near the KC border, an opposing northbound freight developed a hot box and cut journal on one of its hopper cars, resulting in one car derailing and protruding toward the track No. 111 was on. The crews on both trains saw the

car and *The Oklahoman* was trying to stop when it "barely hit" the hopper car. No one was hurt, but wrecking crews from both Frisco and the Santa Fe spent the better part of a weekend getting "Cavalcade" back on the rails. *Above:* Some Chicago & North Western foremen ponder the cleanup progress of a wreck at River Forest, Illinois, after a cut journal resulted in a good-sized pileup. Ho hum.

The etched contours of today's railroads are pictured on this spread. *Above:* A pair of Union Pacific GE diesels roar west toward a setting sun at Loring, Kansas, "stopped" by the camera at $\frac{1}{1000}$ a second. *Opposite:* A four-car train of Jersey Arrow MU cars rolls across the Raritan River drawbridge at Amboy, New Jersey en route to New York City.

Two of Galveston Wharves Electro Motive SW-1 switchers have completed their chores and will wait out the night for another day's work over the railroad's 43.3 miles of tracks around the piers and industries on Galveston Island, Texas.

A Rock Island GP-40 with a UP mate powers a westbound freight out of Bonner Springs, Kansas. To the right, a track car signal indicator; in the background, Santa Fe's bridge across the Kaw River.

Here's one for you, Karl! On this spread, nothing more than the awesome spectacle of Norfolk & Western's biggest-in-steam working a coal train up Blue Ridge in Virginia.

The road engine is a single-expansion class A articulated; the helper, a class Y-6b compound mallet. That's fancy talk for about as much power as a train's drawbars and couplers can take!

Opposite: I came across this location along the Southern Pacific north of Watsonville Junction in the central part of California and fell in love with the setting. There was a wonderfully clean breeze over a world of golden grass—away from freeways, malls, and houses. I discovered that the mystic loveliness of my childhood could even be found in California. The privately re-created Southern Pacific *Daylight* appeared around the bend, headed north, and I have selected a distant shot of her—to complement the surrounding landscape, and to impart the excitement of the train's approach. *Above:* The beautiful train is pictured again, below Salinas, en route to San Francisco.

Winter is quick to seize the airports, highways, and waterways in its inexorable grip, and it is in such deplorable weather conditions that we often remember that the railroads keep running. There are enough trains on the busy four-track ex–New Haven mainline at Noroton Heights, Connecticut, to keep the tracks clear. An Amtrak GG-1 electric shows how it's done—on time!

On this page the Green Mountain Railroad has to resort to harder means, shoving its venerable 1924 Russell wooden plow # 104 south of Mt. Holly, Vermont, on a flat stretch of track known to the railroad employees as "the top of the world." In the mountains and rock cuts, the plow earns its keep, breaking through the drifts.

Above: A dwarf signal—some railroads call 'em pots or jacks—stands in the weeds at Bridge 60 interlocking along the former DL&W in Scranton, Pennsylvania. In railroad operations, a lunar white signal usually indicates a yard switch set for the lead. *Opposite:* Across the country, and far from any yard limits, one of Southern Pacific's unique and powerful SD40T-2 tunnel motors heads four EMD sisters into the twisting horseshoe curves at Bealville, California, in their quest to conquer the Tehachapi Mountains; they are working an eastbound container train. This is springtime in the Tehachapis, but it is desert country that seldom sees rain.

Monochromatic color seems to be very much in sympathy with the cold steel world of railroading. When lighting conditions permit subtle hues and lots of detail, the "true color" of steam railroading really shows, as I feel these two images do. *Above:* The mighty steam locomotive is tended to, in preparation for its run. The hot steam and color of the grease on this ex–Canadian Pacific G-5 show up in warm contrast. *Opposite:* A general "railroady view" of Baltimore & Ohio's yard and facilities at Willard, Ohio. The T-3 class 4-8-2s await their assignments while a switcher classifies cars, tossing her smokey calling card into the sky.

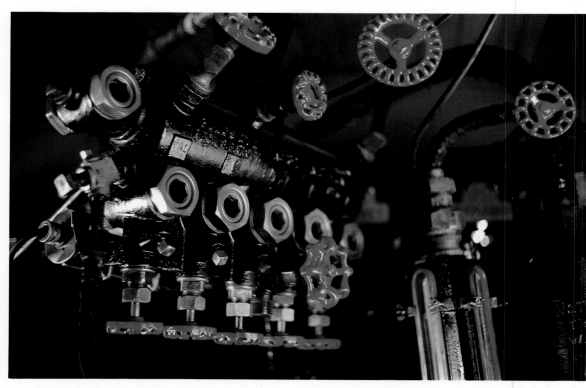

The steam locomotive is a wonderful, fascinating array of machinery—inside and out! *Above:* A close-up look at the hydrostatic lubricator and water glass on the fireman's side of ex–Texas & Pacific 2-10-4 Texas type #610. Basically, oil is distributed through the steam so that a film is deposited on all rubbing surfaces. *Opposite:* Using steam from Steamtown's G-5 locomotive #1246 (second from right) a simulated engine terminal scene is created at Steamtown, Bellows Falls, Vermont. High-pressure steam hoses were run off the 1246 through the other locomotives, which were cosmetically restored and electrically wired up for house power. Jim Boyd of *Railfan* magazine provided the lighting.

Ask someone who *knows* railroading where the best place to watch a train is. Chances are, you'll be told a "diamond," or interlocking tower, where one railroad crosses another. Nowhere on a railroad is the steel-on-steel drama played out more dramatically! Inside the tower, there is the chatter over the radio, the electronic bell or buzzer of approaching trains, the crashing of levers as the operator lines up the right switches. Outside, two honks on the horn from the engineer as three Union Pacific E-units accelerate past BW tower at Bonner Springs, Kansas, with the westbound *Portland Rose*, banging away at the Santa Fe's iron.

A little over twenty-one miles west of BW Tower it is a dreary, dark, dismal day which reduces depth and form, greatly increasing the two-dimensional flatness of a picture, yet the dim light offers an unusual chance to add mood and "feel" to a photograph not otherwise possible to achieve. In the poorest light, three Union Pacific chickenwire F-3s roar westward through Lawrence, Kansas under a tornado-threatening sky. With an ASA of 12, the blurred train is to be expected, along with the subtle colors.

Two quotes from the late Lucias Beebe are very appropriate here: ". . .the architecture of the monstrous and oppressive cast portentous shadows." *Above:* A close-up study of a Norfolk and Western elephantine Y-6 at Shaeffer's Crossing in Roanoke, Virginia. *Right:* "The male Valkyrie in a visored cap riding the hurricane of horsepower. . . ." In this case, the white-hatted hogger lets his 4-8-2 rip! The showstopper is Illinois Central's Mountain type #2536 at Kankakee. Green board!

The Missouri Pacific iron west of Hargrave and the endless bounty of the rich table-flat land itself. The clouds tell the story of what's to come: the cumulus clouds are building up like castles, into cumulo-nimbus clouds, by cooler air moving in from the northwest. In less than two hours, the sky will be black, the lightning fearsome, the rain and hail potentially damaging to the wheat. *Opposite:* Missouri Pacific's westbound coal train looms up off the plains at Hargrave, Kansas, the dark General Electric engines and following cars contrasting sharply with the ripe golden wheat. That high circular cirrus cloud will eventually develop into a violent thunder cell, spawning several damaging tornados.

Winter is a way of life on the Chicago, South Shore, and South Bend Railroad, along the southern tip of Lake Michigan. Two typical scenes are *Above:* Little Joe freight motor #802 getting a westbound under way out of West Gary, Indiana, after switching the Georgia Pacific Corporation and *Opposite:* a two-car train en route from Chicago to South Bend, passing through Miller, Indiana.

A vestige of the past; a promise for the future. *Opposite:* And in a hurry to reach the sun country of New Mexico, Arizona, and California, three fast-moving EMDs lead Rock Island's westbound *Imperial* through a curve near Lawrence, Kansas. The paint on the diesels betrays an era of declining passenger service. *Above:* Over in Turner, Kansas, three decades later, one of Santa Fe's hotshot piggyback trains highballs west with containers and trailers for California.

On this spread, two late winter scenes from the world of electric railroading—where catenary and its steel supports are the prime ingredients. *Left:* A cold wintry sun sets over the four-track mainline of the New Haven Railroad, at Cos Cobb, Connecticut. In the background, the generating plant, source of the railroad's 11,000-volt AC lifeblood. *Right:* An ex–Pennsylvania Railroad GG-1, now leased to the state of New Jersey, heads up the Amboy Secondary, en route to the engine facilities at South Amboy, changeover point between electrics and diesels on the New York to Bay Head run.

"When life's gone, one can't see why shape should remain, even for the little time it does"—John Galsworthy. *Above:* The twisted remains of a now-useless baggage car, after the March 1978 fire that destroyed the Stamford, Connecticut shops of the former New Haven. *Right:* In past books, I have singled out Union Pacific's beautiful Pacific #3222 and the important role it played in my life. On December 20, 1954, the horror of seeing her destroyed was played out in front of me in the Armourdale yards in Kansas City. The flame of the bright acetylene torch—tearing into her flesh—was in savage contrast to the dreary, dismal day. In this nightmarish setting of pure hell, I was numb; everything in a world gone mad was beyond my grasp. Only now can I share the experience.

Rail-fanning in the 1980s can turn up unexpected and, in many cases, pleasant surprises; such was the case here, along the old New York Central tracks above Cold Spring, New York. *Above:* Ex–Pennsy E-8 #4248, now the property of N.J. Transit, but leased to the Metro North Commuter Railroad, roars out of one of the double bores through Breakneck Mountain with a train bound for Poughkeepsie. Not so long ago, two, sometimes three, lightning-striped E8s headed New York Central's streamliners to their far-off destinations through these very same tunnels. For those of us who watched the parade of Central's "Great Steel Fleet," the sight and sound of one E8 brings back poignant memories. *Opposite:* A glimpse of the beautiful Hudson Highlands and the Water Level Route of the old New York Central, through the eastbound bore of the rock tunnel.

Opposite: The beautiful golden light of the late winter sun catches two Western Maryland FA diesels and ex–Reading T-1 Northern #2102 in the Hagerstown, Maryland, yards after heading a special over from Baltimore. Both the early diesels and the steamer were backlit relics in the ever-changing world of railroading. *Above:* The sun glints off the well-worn diamond of the Wabash and Illinois Central Railroads at Starn Tower in Springfield, Illinois.

Mountain railroading over California's Tehachapis between Bakersfield and Mojave is a constant succession of trains and helpers grinding upgrade and around curves in their battle to conquer. *Above:* A Santa Fe SD45-2 throws its formidable 3600-horsepower onto the lead, and into the job of moving eastbound tonnage above Bealville. The combined power on this train is over 15,000 horsepower, including the helper on the rear. *Opposite:* The SD45 helper drifts downgrade below Bealville toward Bakersfield where it will again start the push up to the Tehachapi summit on another train.

Nature's view of the railroad. *Above:* And seemingly rail-deep in grass, these melancholy relics of another era now serve United States Sugar for the transportation of sugar beets over the Southern Pacfic in California. The train is passing through Davis, California. *Opposite:* In contrast to the pastoral simplicities of wooden cars and potatoes, Lackawanna Railroad's beautiful cement Paulins Kill viaduct at Hainsburg, New Jersey, is pictured from deep within the surrounding woods. This magnificent bridge is a quarter-mile long, 115 feet high, and is considered to be one of the most beautiful structures in the world. It was completed in 1910 to cross the Paulins Kill River and the Susquehanna Railroad and Lehigh and New England Railroad.

Not quite the Canadian Pacific's showcase mainline between Montreal and Toronto—rather the once-every-six-months appearance of a load of coal for the heating boiler at the Thomas Turner Paper Mill at Bellows Falls, Vermont. "Careful now you guys with your GP-35s, that's 80 pound Dudley rail under your wheels!" In actuality this is a B&M train with pool power on ex-Rutland rails—wherever *they* are. *Opposite:* And perhaps worse off than the old Rutland, nature starts to take over the abandoned Rock Island main near Lee's Summit, Missouri.

Opposite: If noise could be photographed, this would be it! Union Pacific's mighty three-cylindered, 4-12-2 type #9080 roars into the task of moving a mile of reefers out of Armourdale Yard, Kansas City, bound for Grand Island, Nebraska. The clear, low sun brings out the details, adding drama to an already dramatic departure. *Above:* The ancient order board on the old woodframe depot at Bonner Springs, Kansas, long inoperative, is now a melancholy relic of days gone by, when railroading along the Santa Fe through town was more important.

The "male Valkyrie—in a visored cap riding the hurricane of horsepower that strained behind the stay bolts of the backhead"—Lucias Beebe. *Above:* Southern Railway's steam locomotive #4501 flashes down the mainline through Clifton, Virginia. The view is from the fireman's cushions, on the left side of the cab, watching engineer Cliff Maddox doing the honors. *Opposite:* One of those incredibly crisp, beautiful Vermont summer days—and along come Charlie and Seth, hell bent to change the weather a bit, heading Steamtown's midday train across the flat farm country just out of Chester. The southbound train is pictured approaching Giles crossing. It is doubtful whether the whistle was needed to warn any would-be motorists from crossing in front of the train.

The complete little train, known by many names, such as motor train, doodlebug, gas buggie, and the like, pauses at Versailles, Missouri, on its 118.5-mile journey from Eldon to K.C. With the head-end business almost taken care of, the conductor looks over his charge, much like an airline pilot does his plane before takeoff.

Also taken on the Rock Island Lines, the venerable old depot at Fairview, Kansas, waits out the rain for the daily freight between Horton and Ruskin. Like the doodlebug, Fairview's depot will soon pass from the American countryside.

When the sun rises and sets, it is naturally a warmer color than at any other time of day since, at such a low angle, its rays have to travel through more atmosphere. The resulting diffusion usually results in colors that seem to envelop and glow. *Opposite:* Burlington's great 0-5 class locomotive being readied for a run appears as a silhouette, but her enveloping steam picks up the beautiful pastels of the sunrise at Cicero yard near Chicago. *Above:* At the end of the day the closed-down New Jersey Zinc Mill at Palmerton, Pennsylvania, is tinged by late afternoon's light and the red-gold hue of the setting sun. The contrast of the harsh midday colors would have taken away many of the warm rust hues and weathering that tells the story of shut-down machinery and the start of nature's takeover.

The moods and mysteries of an engine terminal after dark are found in Nickel Plate's vast roundhouse and servicing complex at Belleview, Ohio. *Left:* The dark bulk of Berkshire #742 as she heads for the roundhouse after her nocturnal run. *Right:* In the shadows, three of the big Berks await their assignments out on the mainline.

The old joke in Arizona is that the two great forces pulling on the state are California and Texas. Early one morning in Wilcox, Arizona, I was convinced the hogger on a California-bound pig train—out of El Paso—was trying to drive home the point. Even through the telephoto lens, it appeared the engineer was mercilessly pushing the hell out of the diesels, preparing to tear Wilcox apart, heading to California. Whatever the track speed was, this man was flying a little higher! *Right:* And since I talked so much about the *Rio Grande Zephyr* in the text, I will keep the comment short, except to say rarely did this closely watched train pass through the rugged Rockies unphotographed or unwatched. 4-W drive vehicles, backpacks, and stout hearts made *Zephyr* picture-taking possible!

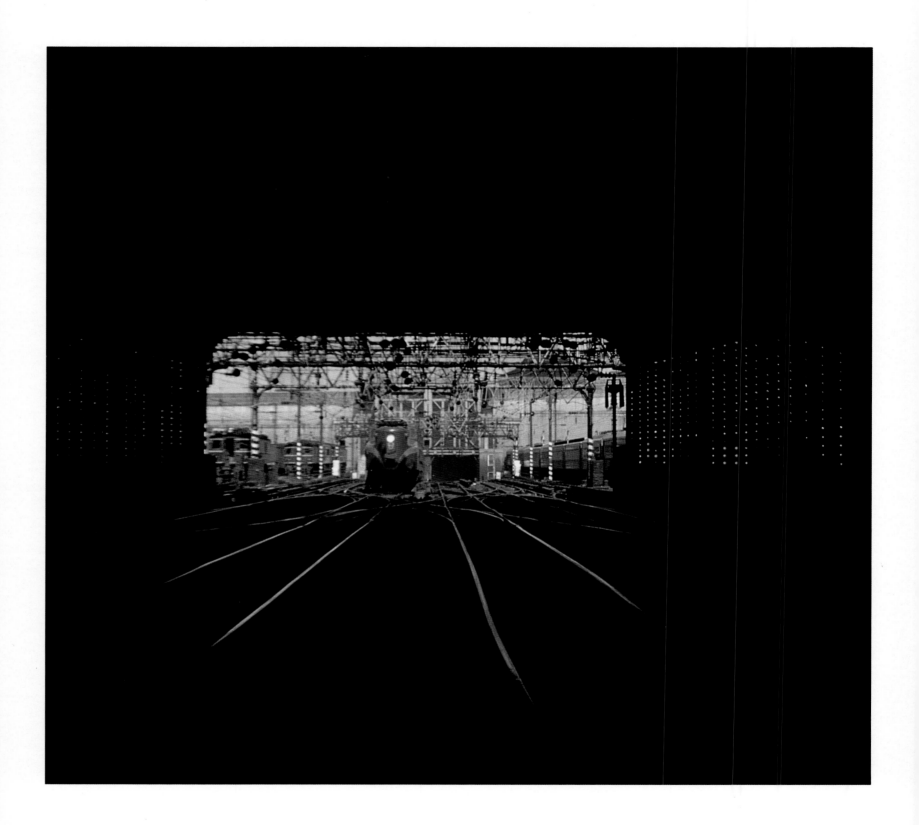

Opposite: Pennsylvania Railroad's Tuscan red GG-1 electric #4909 momentarily bursts into sunshine between the post office and Pennsylvania Station in New York City with the inbound *Spirit of St. Louis.* On the left is New Haven's motor storage track, known as A yard, on the right, Long Island's MU storage tracks. *Above:* The tower operators' view of westbound Connecticut DOT M-2s rumbling across the Norwalk draw, bound for New York City.

Sleeping giants of another era silently drowse away their remaining years in the cold stalls of the Bessemer & Lake Erie Railroad roundhouse in Greenville, Pennsylvania.

Time is arunnin' out for Boston and Maine's hearty Yankee Moguls and Pacifics of the Boston Engine Terminal. Tonight, they will head their commuter trains, but their tomorrows are numbered. *Opposite:* In a blizzard setting looking more like New England, a Santa Fe sectionman tends to thawing switches and lighting propane switch heaters near AY tower in the Argentine yards at Kansas City, Kansas.

Chicago and North Western's *Streamliner "400"* heads out from under the dark steel confines of C&NW's Chicago station en route to Milwaukee and Green Bay. The E-8 diesel hits the low afternoon sun, and for a moment appears to be under a spotlight.

A Peoria & Pekin Union freight rumbles through the Strauss Bascule lift and across the deck plate girder bridge over the Illinois River at East Peoria, Illinois, with cars for the Rock Island and Burlington Northern.

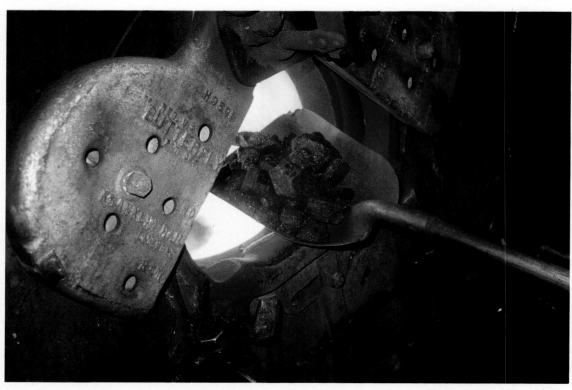

The steam locomotive is a marvelous metal beast that has often been referred to as a "fire-breathing monster." The cab is nothing more than a box bolted to the back of a horizontal furnace that hurtles down two rails on wheels, connected by rods and cylinders that produce the power of harnessed steam. *Above:* Southern Railway's 63′-drivered freight engine #4501 is on the mainline between Alexandria and Manassas, Virginia, and both fireman and scoop are kept busy keeping up steam and speed with a fan trip special. Hand firing coal through the fire doors from a bouncing deck is an art acquired only through years of practice. *Opposite:* Canadian National's Northern-type locomotive #6218 is pictured on a windy night in Grand Trunk Western's Elsdon yard south of Chicago, ready to take a special to Valpariso, Indiana, in the morning.

Aspects of railroading as familiar and important as locomotives and trains are the signals and orders so necessary to operate the railroad. *Opposite:* ¹/₁₀₀₀th of a second stops the Canadian Pacific Alco C-424 heading Boston & Maine's northbound hotshot SPCP past a high green at Claremont Junction, New Hampshire. *Above:* In a somewhat quieter setting, the operator's view overlooking the crossing of the Missouri Pacific and Toledo, Peoria & Western at Watseka, Illinois, the familiar train orders and manifest printouts backlit by the sunshine.

Above: The soft light of autumn filters down upon the old abandoned track of the Ulster & Delaware Railroad over the Esopus Creek east of Phoenicia, New York—the thunder through the woods now coming from nearby Highway 28. *Opposite:* Far from the tranquility of the mountain woods and the unused 90-pound rail over the Esopus Creek, Nickel Plate Road's Berkshire #759 races west with a long freight near Spriggsboro, Indiana. So often we hear slogans promoting something, slogans which we feel are little more than "Madison Avenue gimmickry." I'm happy to say this was not the case with Nickel Plate, whose cabooses and freight advertising were emblazoned with their "High Speed Service" logo. The #759 is a splendid example.

Opposite: Steamtown's ex–Canadian Pacific locomotive #1246 steams past, en route to Chester, Vermont, with "a freight train of memories" dating back to the Golden Age of Steam—the misty steam exhaust from the passing engine momentarily soaks up the low golden light of the late afternoon sun adding to the drama. *Above:* A fearsome storm rages through the Rockies with shafts of unexpected sun occasionally beaming through the boiling, fast-moving black clouds. With lightning dancing around, two openings in the clouds suddenly highlight the nearby 40-foot boxcar, switch stand, and the stand of trees next to the cattle fence. In seconds, the land will fall dark and nearby Glenwood Springs will be drenched—along with myself, the camera, and this part of the Rio Grande Railroad!

Santa Fe's warbonnet paint scheme to many, if not most, is considered to be the most successful of all railroad paint schemes. The Alco PA diesel to many, if not most, is considered to be the most handsome of diesels. Santa Fe's PA #70 is pictured at Los Angeles Union Passenger Terminal in resigned composure. *Opposite:* a close-up glimpse of a Lehigh Valley Alco Century-628 and, more correctly, its oil-filter tank and strainer for conditioning oil for the engine. Fire extinguishers were carried on diesels— usually out of sight, and rarely used.

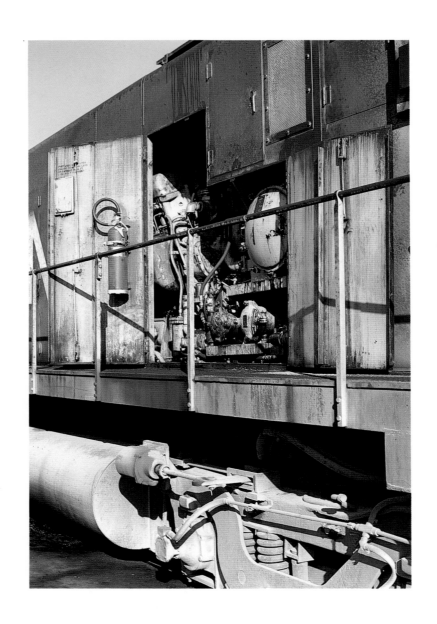

Images of "railroading between runs" can be as interesting as the action of railroading. As evidence, I introduce the two pictures on this spread. *Opposite:* A look at one of the Chicago, South Shore & South Bend Railroad's passenger cars in the quiet of midday at Randolph Street Station, Chicago. The South Shore was slow to discard the old ways. *Above:* The open smoke-box door of ex–Nickel Plate Berkshire #765, during a cleaning and washout at East Peoria, Illinois.

Track patterns. *Opposite:* One of Illinois Central's beautifully proportioned—beautifully fired—2-8-2s gets a stock and reefer train under way out of Maumee, Illinois, in lieu of two black GP-7 diesels that fell down on the job. *Above:* A track inspector walks the amazing complex (or is it complex maze?) of Kansas City Terminal trackage known as "the gooseneck," below KC's Broadway Bridge overpass.

Eternal sunset. The orders are cut, and today Canadian National's big T-2-a class 2-10-2 freight locomotive #4130 is awakened from its sleep and hauled out of the dark Turcot roundhouse in Montreal on the first lap to the scrap yard. The little 0-6-0 puffs mightily, moving the big, stiff engine. In a few weeks, the scene will be repeated, though less dramatically, when a newer diesel will pull #7470 on the first lap to its final destination.

On opposite sides of the continent, a Western Pacific freight heads out of Oroville, California, for the climb over the High Sierras. The intense California sun, filtered by high, thin clouds, is backlit just enough to silhouette the train and not bleach out the golden grass. *Opposite:* Central Vermont's RS-18 Alco #3609 smokes it up, rushing the *Rocket* piggybacker south through Westminster, Vermont.

A close-up look at the enduring, art deco "Indian warbonnet" paint scheme of the Santa Fe; in this case, freshly shopped E-6 number 15 on the *Kansas Cityan* at Lawrence, Kansas. *Opposite:* F-units in the classic ABBA lash-up leading the *Texas Chief* out of Ft. Worth, past Tower 55 at T&P Junction.

Dreaming up, and engineering the move of Steamtown to Scranton, Pennsylvania, was, professionally, the most thankless task I've done to date. The reward for me, personally, however, was at trackside, seeing a dream manifested, as two operating locomotives from Vermont pounded along the mainline of the old DL&W up along the Roaring Brook, telling those around what the Age of Steam was all about. *Opposite:* The 1246 and *Above:* the 2317 (assisting the 1246 on a heavy train) are pictured on different days, eastbound out of Scranton, heading toward Elmhurst.

The lights in the crew shantys add little warmth to this raw day in the Norfolk and Western's Iaeger, West Virginia yards. One of Norfolk and Western's monstrous Y6 class articulateds suggests a rather sinister presence in the quiet snow, the hostler obviously building up the fire to keep it hot for the morning's mine run.

The age of technology is here, along with the twilight of Industrial Smokestack America, and as we rush toward the twenty-first century, much that was once commonplace working America has vanished from the landscape. Consider the railroaders from the age of steam—men I once called a special breed of lordly, grimy heroes like the army of railroaders who kept the great steam locomotives of the Baltimore & Ohio out on on the railroad, such as those pictured at Connesville, Pennsylvania. Only in pictures will they be remembered.

Images from the age of steam appear on this spread, though both shots were taken of, and inside preserved locomotives. *Opposite:* The side-rod, crank pin, and retaining nut on the wheel of ex–Texas & Pacific 2-10-4 locomotive #610. *Above:* Engineer Charlie Millard carefully checks the fire he will be working with on ex–Canadian Pacific 4-6-2 #1246 before leaving Riverside, Vermont, for Chester.

Contrast in railroading: The soft hues of an old Central Vermont boxcar temporarily halted from its journeys on a siding in Brattleboro, Vermont, and the lair of impatient GEs and EMDs in Santa Fe's Argentine, Kansas, yard, waiting for their cross-country assignments.

Above: Two Amtrak GG-1 electrics slam past the Lane substation and its electrical world of transformers, circuit breakers, sectionalizing switches, etc., near Elizabeth, New Jersey, in a frenzied roar of steel-on-steel, hurrying a Florida train toward New York City. *Right:* Two of Frisco's lovely E-8 diesels, named for famous race horses, "Citation" and "Twenty Grand," ease the *Meteor's* equipment through the Terminal Railroad of St. Louis's labyrinth of trackage en route to back the train into the station.

The tried—and the true! *Opposite:* United Aircraft's Turbo Train, while in its short-lived Amtrak service, breezes across the old New Haven's vast Cos Cob draw, ignoring the overhead wires as well as the power plant in the background that is supplying electricity for the 11,000-volt AC electrical system. *Above:* One of Pennsy's magnificent 1930s-era GG-1 electrics reaches for the wires, exciting the Bergen Hill tunnel from Pennsylvania Station, New York, with a Jersey Shore commuter train.

In the early 1960s, Alco came out with its big "Century Series" high-horsepower diesels. The other locomotive builders were in the same game, but the hulking, squarish Alcos were the popular ones with the rail fans. *Opposite:* Lehigh Valley Alco C-628, meet Reading Alco C-424! Both engines are at the large Bethlehem, Pennsylvania engine terminal. *Above:* Union Pacific's hotshot *OKC* roars past the signal on the Midland Curve, heading toward Lawrence, Kansas, and KC behind an array of high-horsepower diesels, including a huge sixteen-wheeled 5,000 h.p. GE U-50.

A close-up look at the important stenciling on a pleasingly weathered 55-ton New York Central hopper car spotted at Cos Cob, Connecticut, with coal for the New Haven Railroad's coal-fired electric generating plant. *Opposite:* A quiet Sunday afternoon at Baltimore & Ohio's Benwood Junction Yard located along the Ohio River near Wheeling, West Virginia. After the Sabbath, this place will become a beehive of activity with the trains returning to the mines on their back-and-forth duties of hauling empties one way and loads the other. That massive EM-1 locomotive in the foreground is assigned to the formidable task of moving coal "over the hump" (the mountains) into Holloway, Ohio.

Above: Durango & Silverton's narrow-gauge Mikado backlights a thousand and one yesterdays, switching cars in Durango, Colorado. *Right:* Chicago, Burlington & Quincy's famous *Pioneer Zephyr* has showed us thousands of yesterdays after ushering in dieselization back in 1934. Now, and toward the end of her career, she is the local *Mark Twain Zephyr* between St. Louis and Burlington, Iowa. As added insult to injury, she is arriving in Quincy with a baggage car tacked behind her observation car!

Left: Absolute Mecca to so many rail fans in the 1950s was B&O's 28-lever mechanical interlocking tower at Attica Junction, Ohio, which guarded the 90° crossing of the Pennsylvania and Baltimore & Ohio Railroads. The tracks across the foreground are B&O's busy Akron-Chicago Division, as viewed looking north toward Sandusky along Pennsy's Toledo Division between Columbus and the Great Lake coal docks at Sandusky. Up through the mid-fifties, both lines were *loaded* with heavy steam, which bore down on the rod-and-lever tower at all hours of the day. *Above:* Staying with the theme of railroads crossing each other, Santa Fe's inbound *Tulsan* approaches AT&SF Junction in Kansas City, minutes away from its Union Station destination. The Fairbanks Morse diesels approaching in the distance help emphasize the maze of interesting trackage at this favorite location of mine.

On this page, one of those gosh-damn-it-where-am-I-out-in-the-middle-of-nowhere chance encounters with the Missouri Pacific at Seward, Kansas. The Garvey elevator at Seward is full of the bounty from the nearby wheat fields and the MOP has been busy picking up loads and setting off empties. After completing her chores, U-boat #4635 leaves town, heading to Radium and its elevator. *Opposite:* A Boston & Maine Alco S-1 switcher burbles down off the loop into East Deerfield yard with a lone hopper car.

Above: Connecticut Department of Transportation M-2s roll Friday's tired commuters home, eastbound over the Mianus River at Cos Cob, Connecticut, boats moored and waiting for one more weekend of use before the cold weather sets in. *Opposite:* And far from the life-style of most Fairfield County Connecticut commuters, an electrician works on a Lehigh Valley RS-3 at the Bethlehem, Pennsylvania, engine terminal.

To a railroad employee in the mechanical department, a 55-ton open-top hopper car in need of a paint job, and possibly some work to meet interchange requirements; to me, the warm, weathered hues of a New York Central hopper, at Greencastle, Indiana, "fading with dignity." *Opposite:* An array of Southern Pacific diesels raises exhausts high into the desert heat, getting their train under way after going into the passing track to meet a westbound hotshot. The location is Lord only knows, somewhere along Route 10 near the Arizona–New Mexico border.

A good old-fashioned blizzard hits northern New England. By the time Green Mountain Railroad's morning train to Rutland does its work around Chester, the snow will be over the rails. The going will get much tougher once the cars are picked up and the mountains are encountered. The driving will get a bit rough on Route 11, too, over which train XR-1 is about to cross, heading into Chester, Vermont.

These two shots of Steamtown's ex–Canadian Pacific locomotive #2317 entering and leaving Nay Aug Tunnel outside of Scranton are combined to bring you the drama of steam performing in—and out of—one of steam's finest theaters. All of the ingredients are present to make Steamtown the *definitive* railroad museum in America if handled carefully—the locomotives interpreted meaningfully in their natural habitat—the mainline excursion being the "living history" of the museum. Here we witness "scheduled preservation" of steam railroading in the grandest tradition.